From Boarding House to Self Determination

You are holding a reproduction of an original work that is in the public domain in the United States of America, and possibly other countries. You may freely copy and distribute this work as no entity (individual or corporate) has a copyright on the body of the work. This book may contain prior copyright references, and library stamps (as most of these works were scanned from library copies). These have been scanned and retained as part of the historical artifact.

This book may have occasional imperfections such as missing or blurred pages, poor pictures, errant marks, etc. that were either part of the original artifact, or were introduced by the scanning process. We believe this work is culturally important, and despite the imperfections, have elected to bring it back into print as part of our continuing commitment to the preservation of printed works worldwide. We appreciate your understanding of the imperfections in the preservation process, and hope you enjoy this valuable book.

FROM BOARDING HOUSE TO SELF DETERMINATION

Nancy Keenan
Superintendent of Public Instruction
State of Montana

Bob Parsley
Indian Education Specialist

Montana Advisory Council for Indian Education
Norma Bixby, Chairperson

Author
Dr. Willard Bill
Olympia, Washington

Printed: January 1990

The Montana Advisory Council for Indian Education, in cooperation with the Office of Public Instruction, has reprinted this unit to help teachers and students understand the chronology of American Indians and the United States educational system.

This unit was written by Dr. Willard Bill to supplement the curriculum of intermediate and secondary teachers in Washington state. The material is applicable to social studies classes, special events or Indian Studies classes.

Dr Bill has given his approval to duplicate this unit for distribution to public schools in Montana. We would, therefore, like to thank him for allowing us to use his material. We think that it will be a useful resource for teachers and students.

FROM BOARDING SCHOOLS TO SELF DETERMINATION

Table of Contents

	Page
Introductory Statement	1
The Contact Period	1
Missions	2
Treaty Period	4
Allotment Period	10
Meriam Report	12
Legislation	18
Termination Period	21
Contemporary Period	23
Indian Education Act	32
Indian Control of Education	34
Conclusion	37
Indian Education Chronology	38
Define Terms	46
Study Questions	47
Footnotes	49

"FROM BOARDING SCHOOLS TO SELF DETERMINATION"

American Indian and Alaskan Native educational systems were broken as a result of an intrusion process. Traditional oral modes of education consisted of training youth by prayer, storytelling, memory skills, and listening. As the intrusion process swept across North America, the traditional educational format of the Native American was interrupted. Tribal education systems were being broken from time of contact (early 1500s) to at least 1871, which marked the end of the treaty-making process between the United States government and Indian tribes. This unit is devoted to establishing the chronology of American Indian and United States educational system.

The Contact Period

Formal education of the American Indian began during the period following initial, sustained contact with European culture in 1492. Numerous studies and reports have viewed this period within a framework of six organizers: a) Mission Period; b) Treaty Period; c) Allotment Period; d) Meriam Report and the New Deal Period; e) Termination Period; and f) 1960s to current. By reviewing these six periods of time, you will be able to understand how the American Indian educational process has been affected by growth and expansion of the United States.

From initial contact in 1492, the intrusion process caused changes in tribal educational formats. American Indians gradually, often abruptly, lost control of their educational institutions. Native American culture has had a constant struggle since to maintain and regain control of their schools.

Missions

For at least 300 years, the Church played a dominant role in the education of the American Indian, beginning with a Jesuit Mission School for Indians (present day Florida) in 1568. And as early as 1617, King James I called upon Anglican clergy to provide funds for educating "children of these barbarians in Virginia." Eventually, an institution of higher learning did develop, known as the College of William and Mary--"a college for the infidels."[1]

The missionary movement, however, increased after the War of 1812. A religious movement of the early 19th century, known as the Great Awakening, stimulated missionary activity in the United States on behalf of the depressed elements in American society. A Congressional committee in 1818 made the following statement.

> In the present state of our country, one of two things seems to be necessary, either that those sons of the forest should be moralized or exterminated. Humanity would rejoice at the former, but shrink with horror at the latter. Put into the hands of their children, the primer and the hoe, and they will naturally, in time, take hold of the plow.[2]

The following year, in 1819, Congress appropriated $10,000 "for the purpose of providing against the further decline of the Indian tribes . . . and for the introducing among them the habits and arts of civilization." This fund became known as the Civilization Fund, and was in the amount of $10,000 annually. The president could draw money upon this fund to hire teachers and maintain schools. These resources were allocated to the missionary church schools because the government had no other mechanism for educating the Indian population.

By 1825, resources were being provided to thirty-eight church schools. However, most of the funds were coming from the churches themselves. Of the $200,000 spent on schools in 1825, roughly seven percent came from the government, six percent from the tribes, and the rest--eighty-seven percent--from the churches. Even as late as the Civil War, the United States was only allocating $10,000 per year form the Civilization Fund for education. Therefore, 19th century American Indian education was primarily a function of mission schools which were investing resources into the educational process.3 Schools taught in the English language, presenting a problem for both instructors and pupils because students arrived at school speaking their native tongue. Therefore, most of the instruction centered on memorization work which utilized religious instruction with the Bible and Catechism used as textbooks.

Treaty Period

The Treaty Period occurred between 1778 (first treaty signed) to 1871 when the United States negotiated the last treaty. The conclusion of the agreement between the United States and the Delaware Tribe, established the treaty process as the primary legal basis for federal policies in regard to the American Indian. The treaty called for a specific provision for education in the form of a promise by the federal government to provide the tribe with teachers. Today there are at least eighty ratified treaties, negotiated by the federal government with Indian tribes, which provide for educational services. Even those tribes that have treaties which do not contain explicit education provisions, consider themselves entitled to funds for educational programs in return for lands ceded by the tribe or rights-of-way granted for road construction on the reservation.[4]

In 1832, Congress created the position of Commissioner of Indian Affairs. The early commissioners, who were responsible for the education of Indians, perceived the American Indian as barbaric and/or primitive. Their educational policies revolved around controlling and assimulating the Indian. Commissioner L. Lea stated in 1850 that Indians must "resort to agricultural labor or starve." During this period the government began an extensive program in agriculture and manual training, in an attempt to "civilize" the Indian.

During the treaty-making period, both the federal government and Indian tribes reserved certain rights for themselves and gave up something in return. Hence, the term "reservation" came into use. The American Indian tribe ceded over a billion acres of land, and tribes were assured that the federal government would deliver educational services, medical care, and technical and agricultural training. This process ended in 1871, after which time the United States government did not sign into treaties with tribes.

The period following 1871 and continuing through the first quarter of the 20th century was a critical one for the American Indian community. It is this fifty-year span which is generally considered to be the period of time when American Indians lost control of their educational systems. At the end of the 19th century and beginning of the 20th century, the federal government became the dominant agency in educating the American Indian. Typically, Indian treaties called for an obligation by the federal government to provide education to American Indian tribes. The treaty with the Kiowas and Comanches, negotiated in October 1867, read as follows.

> Article 7. In order to insure the civilization of the tribes entering into this treaty, the necessity of education is admitted . . . and they therefore pledge to compel their children, male and female, between the ages of 6 and 16 years, to attend school, and it is hereby made the duty of the agent for said Indians to see that this stipulation is strictly complied with; and the United States agrees that for every 30 children between said ages, who can be induced or compelled to attend school, a house shall be provided, and a teacher competent to teach the elementary branches of an English education shall be furnished . . the provisions of this article to continue for not less than 20 years.5

Similar provisions were carried out in the Pacific Northwest. Both the Medicine Creek and Point Elliot Treaties, involving a number of Puget Sound Tribes, contained provisions for education.

While the federal government made sweeping commitments to Indian education, Senate appropriations did not increase to cover the cost of treaty obligations. For example, Congress appropriated only $100,000 in 1870 to start providing school facilities. In 1875, there was only one school for all the Kiowas and Comanches, with forty students enrolled out of a school population of about 400. There was little educational assistance for those Indians who did not have treaty obligation By 1875, the best estimates are that 15% of the total Indian student population was actually in school.

By 1876, Congress began making annual general appropriations for education for American Indian education. The first appropriation was $20,000--a small amount, but it was twice as much as had been offered in 1873. This amount increased to $75,000 in 1885, nearly a million and a half dollars by 1890; and to three million dollars by 1900. These resource were a big part of the Bureau of Indian Affairs budget and they were supplemented by special grants for specific commitments to particular tribes, such as the Kiowas and Comanches. It is estimated that if the federal government had lived up to its treaty obligations, it would have been spending in the neighborhood of two and a half million dollars by 1800 (which was the amount spent in 1900). Therefore, even though the appropriations increased, they were not sufficient to meet all obligations.

Most Congressional appropriations were expended for manual training within a BIA boarding school setting. Manual training was the accepted curriculum for Indian schools and was mentioned in an 1878 circular to agents. It stated in part:

> It is the policy of the Department to combine with the ordinary branches of an English education . . . instruction to the boys . . in cultivating the farms and gardens, and also in a sufficient knowledge of the use, not only of agricultural implements, but of ordinary mechanical tools . . . The girls should also be taught all household industrials such as bedmaking, plain cooking, cutting, making and mending garments for both sexes, the work of the dairy, and the proper care of the hours[6]

The government developed, and used extensively, the off-resevation boarding school beginning with the Carlisle Indian Boarding School in 1878 located in Carlisle, Pennsylvania. Carlisle was an outgrowth of the developmental work in Indian education by General Richard Henry Pratt. General Pratt pursued the boarding school concept first for educational reasons, and second because of his belief that American Indians should be civilized and become part of the dominant society. To achieve this end a form of acculturation known as the "outing system" was employed which placed Indians in non-Indian homes for three years following high school to learn the social graces of non-Indian culture. Government subsidies were made to participating families. Pratt believed that by placing youths outside their community an in a dominant society environment the government was educating American Indians and making them Americans.[7]

Carlisle Boarding School operated until 1917, when it was reopened as a military fort for WWI purposes. Another example of a school that has been in operation for a considerable amount of time is the Chemawa Boarding School, Salem, Oregon, which built a new campus in 1979 and celebrated its one-hundredth anniversary in 1980. Chemawa has voluntary attendance, a 9-12 course offering, and draws students from the Pacific Northwest.

The argument for nineteenth century boarding schools was summed up by a superintendent of Indian schools in 1885 who said:

> The barbarian child of barbarian parents spends possibly six of the twenty-four hours of the day in a schoolroom. Here he is taught the rudiments of the books, varied, perhaps, by fragmentary lessons in the good manners of the superior race to which his teacher belongs. He returns, at the close of the school day, to eat and play and sleep after the savage fashion of the race. In the hours spent in school he has not acquired a distaste for the campfire, nor longing for the food, the home life or the ordinary avocations of the white man . . . The day school gives to the Indian child useful information, but does not take him away from the barbarous life and put him into the enjoyment of civilized life--does not take him from the tepee into the house and teach him to appreciate, by experiencing them, the comforts of the white man's civilization.[9]

Not all Indians of this period attended the off-reservation boarding school, even though enrollment was promoted by the BIA. In the 1890s about one quarter of the Indian students were attending day schools. It cost about thirty dollars a year to support a child in day school, and $170 a year in a boarding school, plus transportation for those living off the reservation. The relatively low cost of the day school was a reason that the parochial schools continued to receive financial support from the government during this period. American Indians enrolled in parochial schools, saved the government approximately one-third of the amount it would cost to send them to a boarding school. By 1887, about twenty percent of the 14,300 American Indian students were enrolled in parochial schools.

Allotment Period

The Allotment Period began in the 1880s with the passage of the Dawes Severalty Act of 1887. It provided for land allotment to individual Indians as a means of breaking up the tribal structure and giving the Indians an opportunity for more "civilized" life. The result was a diminishing of Indian holdings by ninety-million acres--from 140 million to nearly fifty million acres--resulting in severe social disorganization. The 1887 legislation was an outgrowth of a movement, that began as early as 1850, to extinguish Indian land titles. Fifty-two separate treaties, from 1853 to 1857, provided the United States government with 174 million acres of Indian land. Each succeeding commissioner of Indian Affairs, with the exception of Francis A. Walker in 1870s, favoer alloting land to individual Indians.

The Allotment Act, a creation of Senator Henry L. Dawes of Massachusetts, was passed in 1887 with the intent to assimilate the Indians by giving them individual ownership of land, as opposed to the collective land use and possession practiced by most Indian groups. Under the plan, small pieces of tribal land ranging from forty to one hundred and sixty acres were alloted to Indian families or individuals. One provision of the Allotment Act, similar to the Homestead Act, stated Indians, if he/she were adjudged "competent" within twenty-five years, would be given the land to use as he/she saw fit. He would also acquire full citizenship status. The result of this allotment policy was that individual Indians were able to get the land individually in less than twenty-five years. This action was expedited by the passage of the Burke Act of 1906 which allowed them to acquire ownership at once. Then Indians would often sell their land to non-Indians who had the financial means and business abilities to develop the land.

As the new landowners sold or rented individual parcels of land, it tended to increase their dependence on the federal government. American Indians frequently lost their land because they did not charge sufficient rent to maintain it, or they sold their property and exhausted funds from the sale. As Indian owners lost their land, they once again had to turn to the federal government for assistance. The transition from a tribal system to an individual use of the land caused Indians to become further dependent on the United States and the Department of the Interior.

Meriam Report

This section of this unit focuses on the 1928 Meriam Report and the New Deal Period of the 1930s. The Meriam Report was a survey of social and economic conditions of the American Indian conducted by the Brookings Institution of Washington, D.C., which was known as the Institute for Governmental Research. The report was conducted by Dr. Louis Meriam, University of Chicago. Two of the major findings of the report were that: a) Indians were excluded from management of their own affairs, and b) Indians were receiving a poor quality of services (especially health and education) from public officials who were supposed to be serving their needs.

The report was extremely critical of the Bureau of Indian Affairs educational system, but it fell short of advocating the closure of the boarding schools. If the BIA had closed the boarding schools in the 1920s, many Indian young people would have been excluded from education, because they lived in rural areas far from public schools. The report did recommend a change in BIA curriculum.

The educational format was attacked particularly by W. Carson Ryun of Swathmore who wrote the reports' educational section. As a man influenced by the progressive education movement of John Dewey, he was extremely critical of the Bureau's program, which could be called anything but forward thinking. First, he stated the boarding school curriculum did not meet the educational needs of the Indian child. The BIA was teaching a standard curriculum known as the Uniform Course of Study. This program was regimented to the extent that all Indian children throughout the United

States studied the same section of the curriculum daily. Ryun believed this kind of curriculum was not appropriate to meet students' need in view of the diversity of the languages and cultures of the various American Indian tribes.

Secondly, Ryun attacked the age level of the BIA boarding school children. The Meriam Report recommended that the boarding school be reserved for older children and the pre-adolescent children should be eliminated from the boarding school. The proper atmosphere or environment should be a school located in the Indian children's community and near their home. A community school concept in the form of a day school for the youngster that would function as a community center, and serve the entire Indian culture, rather than just the school-age youngsters. Under this plan, the children would not go to boarding school until they were old enough to learn a trade, and following this training, they would seek employment.

Another area of criticism was that the vocational training was outmoded and not realistic to meet the needs of the world of work. Trades studied in the curriculum were vanishing in the workplace, and they were not taught at a sufficient skill level to enable the student to gain employment. Even if the training had been adequate, it was not preparing the student for a job located on or near reservations. Training did not encourage the student to return to the reservation where his/her skills and human resources could be used to the benefit of the tribe.

The Meriam Report became an indictment of assimilationist policies which had existed for at least fifty years within the Bureau of Indian Affairs school system prior to 1928. The report stated that the purpose of the Bureau of Indian Affairs should be to educate Indian youths to function in both worlds--the white world and the Indian world. The primary task of the Bureau should have been the education of, and not the assimilation or socialization of, the Indian child. The Meriam Report became the definitive Indian education study of the first half of the 20th century, and it was an indictment of the fifty years of federal domination in educating American Indians via the BIA

Charles J. Rhoads became the first Indian commissioner to base operations upon the Meriam Report recommendations. Rhoads was appointed Commissioner in 1929 by President Hoover, and seemed well-equipped to work within the framework of the Meriam Report recommendations. He was a wealthy Quaker who had a concern for the American Indian and was President of the Indian Rights Association, founded in 1882. He was supported politically by the Secretary of the Interior. The New York Times also provided support when it stated that it was time to reorganize the Bureau which "had obsolete traditions, methods, and standards and its obfuscated Washington officials." Rhoads meant to provide reforms, but the fall of the stock market and the resultant depression worked against increases in appropriations for American Indian education. Rhoads provided a transition from the pre-Meriam Report policies to the progressive administration (1933-45) of John Collier. During his term between 1928 and 1933, the off-reservation boarding schools decreased from seventy-seven to sixty-five, but the schools' population increased because of economic necessities of Indian families, brought on by the depression.

With the 1932 election of Franklin Delano Roosevelt as President of the United States, an important decision was to be made as to selecting the Bureau of Indian Affairs Commissioner. If the person selected was not in agreement with the recommended Meriam Report reforms, and the initial work carried on by Rhoads, Indian education could have been set back many years. When the Roosevelt victory was announced, a number of concerned people, including John Collier, sent a petition to the president with over six hundred signatures including educators, clergy, physicians, social workers, and others. They stated "So great is the Indian distress in many tribes, and so rapid is the shrinkage of Indian property held in trust by the government, that we do not believe that we are exaggerating when we suggest that your administration represents almost a last chance for the Indians."9

John Collier was selected to be commissioner of Indian Affairs, which served to advance the cause of Indian education in America. Collier had support for his innovative educational plans from the Secretary of the Interior, Harold Ickes. As Commissioner of Indian Affairs, John Collier was able to carry out recommendations made in the Meriam Report; and he tried to bring the educators within the Bureau of Indian Affairs to a culturally-relevant and realistic approach to American Indian education. In 1936, he appointed Willard Beatty BIA Director of Education. Beatty carried out many reforms, and his educational influence persisted from 1936 to 1952. Beatty was instrumental in establishing a link between schools and students' homes. Initially, he attempted to introduce Indian culture into the boarding school curriculum, although he had a very difficult time getting it accepted by local schools.

The Bureau of Indian Affairs used a definition of "culture" developed by Edward Sapir (professor of Anthropology and Linguistics at Yale from 1931 to 1939). He stated that "genuine culture is . . . the expression of a richly varied and yet somehow unified and consistent attitude toward life, an attitude which sees the significance of any one element of civilization in its relation to all others."10 The Bureau broke Sapir's definition of culture into components--history, customs and tradition, religion, art, language, philosophy, society structure and regulations and a system of values. Only three of these--language, art, and history--were eventually introduced into the Bureau schools.

A reform in bilingual education illustrated the difficulty of implementing instructional innovation within the Bureau of Indian Affairs schools. First, there was hostility within the Bureau toward Native American languages. Prior to the Meriam Report, not only was English used as the only language of instruction, but Indian children were forbidden to use their own native languages at the Bureau of Indian Affairs schools. Violaters of this rule were physically punished, and in all cases discouraged from using their native language In the words of Commissioner J.D.C. Atkins, "if the language was good enough for a white man or a black man, it ought to be good enough for a red man."11

This negative attitude toward Native American languages carried over to the Collier administration; and even though the official policy changed, the actions of the Bureau personnel did not. Bureau teachers and administrators, who had been with the agency, continued to treat Indian languages in a negative manner Reluctant employees made implementation of bilingual innovations very difficult.

A second problem was the lack of competent instructors to teach bilingual education. Many of the teachers, hired prior to Collier, were poorly trained, knew little about Indian culture, and had no language training. Teacher standards were raised under Commissioner Rhoads, but personnel available to John Collier were not adequately trained in Native

American languages to provide instruction. Teachers were hired on the basis of passing Civil Service examinations and were sent off to teach in the boarding schools, even though they may never have seen an Indian person in their lives.

A third curricular problem was the scarcity of American Indian and Alaskan Native bilingual books. Books typically contained little information about the Native American, and were written in English. Willard Beatty, Director of Education, addressed this problem by producing bilingual materials at Haskill Institute. Lack of bilingual instructional materials continued to be a problem during the John Collier administration.

Legislation

The foregoing section discussed problems which prevented innovative, creative curriculum development for the American Indian student. Despite the administration of two consecutive commissioners of Indian Affairs who were sympathetic to the Indian cause, the economic distress of the country and Bureau of Indian Affairs personnel attitudes hindered creative innovations within the Department of Interior. One key legislative statute was the Indian Reorganization Act of 1934, which ended the Allotment Period and laid the groundwork for more autonomous tribal government. Referred to as the Wheeler Howard Act, it had a number of important provisions including prohibition of further allotment, establishment of a method for tribal organization, and incorporation. This act has been referred to as the Indian Bill of Rights.

The Johnson-O'Malley (JOM) Act, passed on April 16, 1934, was another important piece of legislation. JOM authorized the Secretary of the Interior to contract with states or territories for the education, medical attention, agricultural assistance, and social welfare of Indians in the state.[12] The legislature expanded the authority of the Secretary of the Interior, allowing him to contract with state or private corporations, agencies or institutions. Funds made available from the Johnson-O'Malley Act were designed to assist in reducing boarding school enrollment and to place Indian students in public schools.

The Johnson-O'Malley legislation recognized that Indians living near or adjacent to non-Indian populations could easily attend local public schools rather than being transported to boarding schools. This provided a mechanism to aid public schools in educating American Indians rather than setting up separate schools. Johnson-O'Malley became a mechanism for the provision of local education rather than in federal off-reservation or on-reservation boarding schools. The Act also facilitated federal and state cooperation by making contracts negotiable at the state level. In 1935, California became the first state to enter into a contract, and by 1940, contracts had been negotiated with the states of Arizona, Minnesota, and Washington.

John Collier and Willard Beatty also introduced another innovation that was particularly needed--American Indian teacher training for Bureau of Indian Affairs teachers. In-service training was extremely popular at the time because it afforded the opportunity to exchange teaching ideas in a setting conducive to learning for the Native American student. Communications during the 1930s had to be conducted by telegraph, letter, or radio, so the idea of meeting in a central location and sharing materials and ideas was popular with the teachers. In-service workshops were conducted at such places as Chemawa, Oregon and Sherman Institute, California. They were popular because of improved interpersonal relations and they became a source of some satisfaction to Beatty, who had recognized the need for staff development in BIA schools.

Prior to becoming Director of Education, Beatty had lengthy talks with anthropologists and Indian Bureau employees to prepare himself. Beatty knew a need existed for improved communication and he had a close relationship with the Progressive Education Association, which allowed him to rely on their wealth of ideas in improving in-service education. Beatty was resisted by the old guard of Bureau employees who felt that educators outside the Bureau had little to offer them in terms of dealing with Indian students. Collier and Beatty were criticized so severely that Homer Howard, who was supervisor of in-service training, had to write letters to the superintendents stressing the importance of these courses for the teachers.

In summary, John Collier's administration was one of tremendous innovation. He started programs in bilingual education, adult basic education, teacher training, Indian culture, and Affirmative Action. He served for twelve years as commissioner; during that time, sixteen boarding schools were closed and eighty-four day schools were opened. He reduced the ratio of Indian students attending boarding schools to those attending day school. Whereas, in 1933, three-fourths of all Indian students were enrolled in boarding schools, by 1943 two-thirds were attending day schools. Many of Jonn Collier's and Willard Beatty's innovations were halted with the entry of the United States into World War II. Political sentiment by the end of World War II began to change the government's attitude towards Indian education.

In the post-World War II era, there was a shift in Beatty's educational program which reflected the rise of a termination movement. Termination stressed eliminating the reservation system and moving Indians to cities. Beatty responded to this idea by encouraging vocational education, which he earlier had discouraged He believed that vocational training would give skills to Indians, which they could use when they left the reservation and moved to urban centers. The educational reforms that had begun under Collier and Beatty in the 1930s gave way to the termination movement of the late 1940s and early 1950s.

Termination Period

The fifth period is often referred to as the termination period. At the close of World War II there was a movement to revert Bureau policies to a prior era. The U.S. Congress began to use specific language in their deliberations regarding termination. In 1944 a house Select Committee n Indian Affairs offered recommendations for achieving "The final solution of the Indian problem."[13] Once again there was a movement to take Indian children away from their homes and place them in off-reservation boarding schools. The Committee Report stated, "The goal of Indian education should be to make the Indian child a better American, rather than to equip him simply to be a better Indian."[14] By 1948 the Commissioner of Indian Affairs was setting up criteria for determining a tribe's readiness for withdrawing from Federal Services. Dillon Myer became Commissioner in 1950 at a time when the termination policy was well in motion. The termination goal was to have tribes rid themselves of Indian trust land and to terminate federal recognition and services. Indians would leave the reservation and relocate in cities.

The government continued to withdraw services during the 1950s. In 1952 the Bureau of Indian Affairs closed all of its federal school is Idaho, Michigan, Washington, and Wisconsin. Further loans to Indian students authorized under the Reorganization Act of 1934 were discontinued. The next year a number of boarding schools were closed and Indian students were transferred to public schools. Boarding schools that continued to operate returned to the assimilationist policies of the pre-Meriam Report. Students were educated far from their homes. For example, the Navajo children of Arizona were educated at Chemawa Boarding School in Oregon, and Northwest Indians were sent to such schools at Chilloco and Concho boarding schools in Oklahoma.

Other regressive legislation was passed in the 1950s. House Concurrent Resolution 108 of the Eighty-Third Congress in 1953 called for an end to federal services to Indians. Also, a number of Indian bills were introduced between 1953 and 1960 which called for termination. Legislators who introduced these bills included Representative William H. Harrison of Wyoming and Senator Arthur V. Watkins of Utah, who submitted termination resolutions which read, in part:

> It is the policy of Congress as rapidly as possible, to make the Indians within the territorial limits of the United States subject to the same laws and entitled to the same privileges and responsibilities as are applicable to other citizens of the United States, and to grant them all the rights and prerogatives pertaining to American Citizenship.15

The Menominees of Wisconsin became the first tribe slated for termination by the federal government on June 17, 19854. Menominees had an advanced economic development program in the areas of forest land investment and a sawmill operation. Final termination of the Menominees was completed on April 30, 1961. Other tries terminated during this period were the Klamaths--western Oregon Indians, four small bands in Utah; the Alabama Cuocoushattas of Texas, the Ponca tribe of Nebraska, the Uintah and Ourayute mixed bloods of Utah, the Wyandottes, Ottawas, and Peorias of Oklahoma. Now, these functions were given to the states, which used state court systems. This transfer of law enforcement was another indication that termination was vitally affecting American Indian tribes.

Contemporary Period

The contemporary period includes the decades between 1960 and 1980's. A number of studies, reports, and legislation during the 1960s were related to Indian education and were directed toward improving the American Indian educational system. Among these were. a) the Elementary and Secondary Education Act of April 11, 1965, b) Economic Opportunity Act of 1965; c) the joint study of the Departments of the Interior and Health, Education and Welfare, 1966; d) the Coleman report of 1966; e) formation of the National Indian Education Advisory Committee 1966, f) Pennsylvania State Research Conference in 1967, g) Senate Subcommittee on Indian Education 1967; h) Presidential messages of 1968 and 1970; i) Havighurst National Study of Indian Education 1970; j) the Indian Education Act of 1972. All of these factors coupled with the civil rights movement of the 1960s created a need for American Indian/Alaskan Native access to education

Throughout the 1950s and 1960s American Indian leadership moved to formally reject the idea of termination that was proposed and planned by federal government officials during the 1950s. A January 1961 publication entitled, "Funds for the Republic Study" by the Commission on Rights, Liberties and Responsibilities of the American Indian called attention to the injustices of the termination policies, the paternalistic attitudes of the Bureau of Indian Affairs, and the inadequate services provided Indians. It also called for reorganization of the Bureau's education program and increased Indian involvement in determining programs affecting Indians. These ideas were to dominate Indian education during the 1960s.

The Kennedy Administration (1961-63) responded to the American Indian by conducting its own study directed by the Secretary of the Interior, Stewart Udall. In January 1961 a report was issued which called for new activities in Indian education ranging from increasing scholarship funds to encouraging Indian parent participation in the formulation of school programs. The report went on to further repudiate termination and suggested that economic development on Indian reservations be the basis of a new federal Indian policy. As a consequence, between 1961 and 1966 the Bureau of Indian Affairs shifted policy direction and began programs of economic and community development.

A significant legislative development occurred in 1965 with the passage of the Economic Opportunity Act, which gave Indians the opportunity to participate in, and to control, their own programs. For the first time a low-income group in the United States was given funds to administer programs for its own people, and be held accountable for those resources. Other federal programs had significant Indian participation including Headstart, Upward Bound, Job Corps and Vista. The Economic Opportunity Act created the "Community Action Programs," which involved 105 Indian reservations in 17 states by the end of the 1960s. Initiative for a new design of Indian education called the Rough Rock Demonstration School on the Navajo reservation in Arizona was spearheaded by the Office of Economic Opportunity. Rough Rock became a symbol for Indian participation and control, thereby becoming a forerunner of Indian participation in educational decision-making.

The school was established June 27, 1966, and controlled by a five-member Navajo school board. Stanford Dravitz and Dr. Robert Roessel were two of the prime movers behind the school's creation. Dr. Roessel outlined the concepts that were to guide the Rough Rock education process:

1) Indians would never give schools their wholehearted moral support until they were involved significantly as adults and given a measure of control. 2) English must be taught as a second language to Indian children, not regarded as something they could learn immediately through mere exposure. 3) The school should be responsible, not only for educating Indian children, but for assisting in the development of local communities, through extensive adult education opportunities and other means. 4) The schools should help transmit to the young the cultures of their parents, tribal elders should be used by the schools, for instance, to teach traditional materials.[16]

Regarding teachers and their pre-service training Dr. Roessell stated the following before the Senate Indian Education Subcommittee:

It is extremely important for the teachers . . . to understand the culture, language, and the family life of the children they are involved in educating. There are a number of institutions that have developed specific and complete programs, in at least one instance leading to a masters degree, for teachers working with Indian children. This approach must be expanded.[17]

Further in his testimony he spoke for the need to implement required courses in Indian Education. Dr. Roessel's statement is applicable in all parts of the United States.

> I certainly should like to see the day when such states as
> Arizona and New Mexico, where you have the largest concentration
> of Indian population in the nation, require teachers who teach
> Indians to have a certificate which indicates they have had
> minimal number of courses in Indian education.18

Another significant point of the 1960s was the passage of the Elementary and Secondary Education Act of 1965. The law stated in generic terms the goal of improving education of disadvantaged children. Indian communities become involved in this program, and by 1969 approximately nine million dollars were appropriated specifically for Indians in federal schools. The Act made it a national policy and priority that all disadvantaged children in the country would have an effective education. Title I of the Act provided for millions of dollars to be spent on the disadvantaged youth, and in 1966 the Act was amended to include the Bureau of Indian Affairs. In 1968 five million dollars were allocated. Most, if not all, Indian children benefited from this new legislation due to the formula for allocation.19

Resources were administered by the United States Office of Education (USOE). The Bureau of Indian Affairs had to apply to the U.S. office of Education for funds. By 1969, the money was spent as follows: half the funds was allocated for in-service training, teacher aides and pupil personnel services, and the remainder went to curriculum development, enrichments (field trips), language arts, health and food, kindergarten, mathematics, and science.

The era of the 1960s was begun with important legislation, and the decade ended with presidential messages regarding Indian self-determination. In March of 1968, President Johnson proposed a new goal, which ended the old debate about termination of Indian programs, and stressed self-determination. This goal called for the erasing of old attitudes of paternalism and promoting partnership and self-help. The president stated on March 6, 1968

> I propose a new goal for our Indian programs a goal that ends the debate about "termination" of Indian programs and stresses self-determination; a goal that erases old attitudes of paternalism and promotes partnership self help.20

President Nixon was to follow with some other positive steps subsequent to the administration of President Johnson. Like President Johnson (in 1966 and 1969 Indians were appointed to the office of Commissioner of Indian Affairs), he appointed an Indian as the Commissioner of the Bureau of Indian Affairs. President Nixon also presented a special message to the congress on July 8, 1970 regarding Indian Affairs. The message reaffirmed the historic relationship between the federal government and the Indian communities. It also called for Indian control of federally-funded Indian programs. The president remarked.

> Because termination is morally and legally unacceptable because it produces bad practical results, and because the mere threat of termination tends to discourage greater self-sufficiency among Indian groups, I am asking the congress to pass a new concurrent resolution which would expressly renounce, repudiate, and repeal the termination policy as expressed in House Concurrent Resolution 108 of the 83rd Congress 21

Other recommendations included a new concurrent resolution which would support voluntary Indian control of Indian programs with the necessary technical assistance from the government to facilitate transfer of responsibilities, restore the sacred lands near Blue Lake to the Indians of the Taos Pueblo, support Indian communities in assuming control of Indian schools, establishing Indian school boards, tribal administration of funds, and tribal contracting for the operation of schools; and promote economic development legislation via the Indian Financing Act of 1970, which would enable Indian leaders to arrange for the development and use of natural resources. The first of these to become law was the restoration of the Blue Lake and 48,000 acres of surrounding land to the Taos Pueblo Indians of New Mexico.

Indian education, despite the new directions and new forward thrust, was found to be a failure nationally. The Subcommittee on Indian Education (of the Committee on Labor and Public Welfare of the United States Senate 91st Congress, First Session, chaired by Robert Kennedy and subsequently chaired by Senator Edward Kennedy) noted the complete failure of Indian education in the Senate Report of 1969. As they carried out their investigation they found low quality school buildings, poor course materials in books, negative attitudes of teachers and administrators, and lack of accessibility to school buildings for Indian communities. These facts led them to call Indian education in America a complete failure. A few of the facts they discovered are mentioned as follows

Forty thousand Navajo Indians, nearly a third of the entire tribe, are functional illiterates in English, the average educational level for all Indians under federal supervision was five school years, more than one out of every five Indian men have less than five years of schooling, drop-out rates for Indians were twice the national average, in New Mexico Indian students were walking two miles to take the bus every day and riding 50 miles to school, the average age of top level BIA education administrators was 58 years; in 1953 the BIA began a crash program to improve education for Navajo children. Between then and 1967, supervisory positions in BIA headquarters increased 113%; supervisory positions in BIA schools increased 144%; administrative and clerical positions in BIA schools increased 94% (yet teaching positions increased only 20%). In one school in Oklahoma the study body is 100% Indian yet it is controlled by a three-man, non-Indian school board. Only 18% of the students in federal Indian schools go on to college, with the national average 50%. Only 3% of the Indian students enrolled in college graduate; and the national average is 35%. The Bureau of Indian Affairs spent only $18 per year per child on textbooks and supplies, compared to the national average of $40, only one of every hundred Indian college graduates will receive a Masters Degree and despite a Presidential directive of 1967, only one of the 226 BIA schools was governed by an elective school board.22

The 1969 Kennedy Report filled seven volumes with testimony by Indian educators and other Indian education experts on the achievement level of Indian education in America. Their conclusions were an indictment of American Indian education in the United States. The Senate used the Meriam Report of 1928 as a benchmark and noted the failure of American Indian education between 1928-1968. This Senate Report was more limited in its objective than the Meriam Report, but it had national impact because Indian leadership had become more politically active since 1950 and they recognized that, in order to change their educational system, they would have to take more control. In the long run, the Kennedy Report may have had more lasting implications for national changes in Indian education than the Meriam Report had.

Another study of this time period should be mentioned. A national study of American Indian education was carried out by Estelle Fuchs and Robert J. Havighurst. This study was done under a contract with the U.S. Office of Education and was completed in 1971. The study was carried out between the years of 1967 and 1971 and was conducted by utilizing eight university centers: the University of Arizona, the University of Chicago, the University of Colorado, the University of Minnesota, North Carolina State University, Oklahoma State University, Pennsylvania State University and San Francisco State College. The research investigated how Indian people perceived education, and to examine relationships between Indian and school communities throughout the United States.

The Havighurst Study noted that by 1970 there was a much clearer government policy on Indian Affairs than there had been in the previous decade. Even though there had been much positive change in the Kennedy Administration in the early 1960s, the Udall Report was conceived as being somewhat ambiguous, and sidestepping the termination issue. By the end of 1969, the subsequent Kennedy Report stripped away all pretentions from both public and boarding school systems of their education of the Indian youth, by 1970, issues had clarified at the national level. Other agencies besides the Bureau of Indian Affairs were involved in programs to assist the American Indian, including the Office of Economic Opportunity, United States Office of Education (USOE), the Department of Housing and Urban Development (HUD), the Department of Labor, and the Public Health Service.

Further, the Bureau of Indian Affairs had expanded its services into areas of education, vocational training, housing, and industrial and community development. There had been two speeches (1968/1970) by Presidents Johnson and Nixon indicating the policy of the government would be to further Indian selfdetermination. The report was written at a time when there was an increasing shift to Indian self-determination in education.

Indian Education Act

In 1972 the Indian Education Act, P.L. 92-318, was passed by the United States Congress with an initial appropriation of $18 million. By fiscal year 1987 the Office of Indian Education had an appropriation of $67 million. This amount was allocated to carry out provisions of the Indian Education Act. These funds were divided between Parts A, B, and C of the legislation.

A major portion of the funds were directed toward Part A, which is allocated to the public school districts.

Part B was entitled, "Special Programs and Projects to Improve Educational Opportunities for Indian Children " This was an amendment to Title Eight of the Elementary and Secondary Education Act of 1965. These funds could be allocated for such things as planning, pilot and demonstration projects providing educational services to Indian children, development of exemplary educational programs, pre-service and in-serivce training programs, and the dissemination of information materials to the Indian community.

Funds under Part B are discretionary and are allocated to state and local education agencies (LEA's), Indian tribes and organizations, and institutions of higher education.

Fellowships are also granted under Part B for American Indians and Alaskan Natives seeking a professional degree for careers in medicine, law, engineering, forestry, and business. The fellowship program has developed in the 1970s as the main source of graduate funds for Native Americans in the United States. The Bureau of Indian Affairs does not have a similar program.

Adult education programs are awarded from Part C, which makes grants to state and local education agencies and Indian tribes and organizations.

Part D of the legislation created the Office of Indian Education with the administration conducted by the Deputy Commissioner for Indian Education. This position has been administered by Dr. Wm. Demmert and Dr. Gerald Gipp during the 1970s.

Indian Control of Education

Educational innovations which had their impetus in the 1960s found their fruition in the 1970s. Indian communities and Alaskan villages began to develop their own educational programs open to enrollment by native American youth. These schools were few in number at the beginning of the 1970s. The coalition of Indian-controlled school boards had approximately four member schools in the early 1970s, but over 150 members by 1980. This phenomenal growth was the result of several factors.

Throughout the 1960s American Indian and Alaskan Native leadership developed to such an extent that there was a mushrooming expectation that Indian communities could, in fact, realize self-determination.

Indian leaders developed their tribal resources rapidly during the 1970s. Tribal structures became more sophisticated as they used their resources to train their staff, develop the tribal business structure, communicate with national political leadership, and develop long-range plans for tribal self-determination.

Tribal leaders began to transfer the skills gained in resource development to education. In many cases they encouraged their educational leaders to think positively about developing a tribal system which would serve the local community. This idea spread among Indian communities, tribes, and villages. Planning meetings were conducted, surveys administered, and decisions reached to begin the development of school systems to be controlled by American Indians and Alaskan Natives. To the degree that Indian leaders perceived public school systems to be unresponsive, they began to plan for the establishment of tribal schools.

American Indian and Alaskan Native leaders perceived that schools controlled by their community would have a built-in cultural relevance which would strengthen the self-concept of students. After years of struggling to inform elected officials and educators of the unique status of the American Indians they realized that an Indian-controlled school was necessary to provide validity to native culture. The Indian-controlled school, by its very nature of organization, is held accountable to the local Indian leadership.

The teachers and administrators understand their role in enhancing the culture, self-concept, and confidence of Indian youths entrusted to their teaching. With the tribal council or village council in control there is an incentive for the teacher to promote cultural relevance.

Tribal councils and their education committees also realized that they were capable of administering the program even though they had a small student population. The myth that a school system needed a large number of students to have an adequate education program was challenged. Indian educators courageously stepped out to begin instruction, often in cramped quarters, with Indian and Alaskan Native students. The fact that these Indian-controlled schools increased (noted by membership in the Coalition of Indian Controlled School Boards) was evidence that tribal schools were meeting an important need of which Indian tribes had been deprived for the prior one hundred years.

Post-secondary education was included in the educational plans of Indian communities. From 1968 when Navajo Community College was founded, to the present day, Indian communities have developed a variety of schools which are designed to meet educational needs. Schools vary from the Sinte Gleska College at Rosebud, South Dakota, to the Lummi Aquaculture School in Western Washington. They are controlled by the Indian community and provide valuable training to meet the demand for skilled workers in industry, tribal development, social/welfare services, and education. The American Indian Higher Education Consortium emerged as a national organization to facilitate communication between these institutions, develop legislation to provide resources for program operation, and to provide technical assistance to regions of the United States that want to develop Indian-controlled institutions of higher education.

Conclusion

A major conflict between cultures occurred when the federal government attempted to bring American Indians into the mainstream of society following the 1871 conclusion of the treaty-signing period. The boarding school was the primary institution encouraging acculturation of Indian youth due to the schools' adherence to a regime that reflected the military fortifications in which schools were housed. Different conceptions of time and history were taught in boarding schools, and Indian students were confronted with a school culture and curriculum vastly different from their own tribal reality. Students were asked to study history as a progressive development of societies as expressed by the European thought processes rather than a cyclical experience of nature as taught by their elders.

Indian Education Chronology

The following dates and events are listed to highlight events of Indian education. They indicate an increase of Indian control in Indian education which began in the 1960s and continued throughout the 1980s. A significant event in this period was the Economic Opportunity Act of 1964 which, for the first time, granted local communities economic resources for their own management. This concept led the way for local communities to control numerous projects, including education.

1539 Lectures of Francisco de Vitoria at the University of Salamanca, Spain, advocating that Indians were free men and were exempt from slavery. They were to be dealt with through treaties and fair trade.

1619 Virginia Company started the first mission schools which were abandoned in 1622

1803 Three thousand dollars were appropriated to civilize and educate the heathens.

1819 Another appropriation was made to civilize and to educate the Indians. A $10,000 annual appropriation was known as the "civilization fund."

1824 The Bureau of Indian Affairs was established within the War Department.

1831   The Cherokee were forcefully removed from Georgia to Indian territory in Oklahoma. This removal contributed to destroying the educational systems of the Cherokee, Choctaw, Creeks, Chickasaws, and Seminoles.

1849   Gold was discovered in California and the Indian people lost most of their possessions. The Mission Indians in California survived with one-tenth of their former members.

1871   Congress passed legislation ending the treaty-making process   Most treaties contained education provisions for the tribes.

1877   The Board of Indian Commissioners included educational statistics in their annual reports, thus creating a base line for measuring progress of Indian education.

1879   Carlisle Boarding School opens in Carlisle, Pennsylvania.

1880   Chemawa Boarding School opens in Salem, Oregon. This school celebrated its one hundredth birthday in 1980.

1890   Thomas J. Morgan published a code of "Rules for Indian Schools" which indicated that government school was only intended to be a temporary provision to serve Indian students until they could attend white schools. It marked the beginning of the practice of sending certain Indian children to public schools.

1893   Compulsory attendance law passed by Congress for Indians (March 3, 1983, U.S. Stat., Vol. 27, p. 635).

1921 Snyder Act. Placed total responsibility for Indian affairs under the direction of the Secretary of Interior

1924 The Snyder Act made Indians citizens of the United States.

1928 The Brookings Institution published the Meriam Report which was critical of the Bureau of Indian Affairs school system.

1932 John Collier appointed commissioner of the Bureau of Indian Affairs. He served in this position until 1945

1933 Indian Emergency Conservation Works (IECW) program, which provided vocational training to Indians. Eighty-five thousand Indians served in the IECW between 1933 and 1942.

1933 The Board of Indian Commissioners was disbanded by executive order.

1934 Johnson-O'Malley legislation passed to provide funds for Indian students to attend schools nearest their home.

1936 Willard Beatty appointed Director of Indian Education in the BIA. He served in this position until 1952.

1952-60 Legislation introduced to terminate the federal trust relationship between the federal government and Indian tribes.

1961 The National Indian Youth Council was organized.

1964   The American Indian Historical Society was founded in San Francisco, California. This organization was composed of Indian scholars, and they set about to develop accurate scholarly works on the American Indian.

The Economic Opportunity Act was passed. It provided for Indian control of federal funds. Among the many projects funded were Headstart, Job Corps, Vista, and Indian community action programs.

1965   Elementary and Secondary Education Act. This act was passed in the initial years of President Johnson's administration. It was to reach all disadvantaged youth in the United States. The Bureau of Indian Affairs was included in the legislation in 1966.

1966   First Indian Teacher Corps projects began at Niabrara, Macy and Winnebag, Nebraska.

Rough Rock Demonstration School opened on the Navajo Nation at Chinle, Arizona, under the control of an elected Navajo Board of Education.

1957   The Bureau of Indian Affairs established the National Indian Education Advisory Committee.

1968   Senator Robert F. Kennedy, Massachusetts Democrat, begins Senate probe into Indian education.

First all-Indian Teacher Corps projects begun in Arizona, Wisconsin, Wyoming, Alaska, Minnesota, Montana, North Dakota, South Dakota, and

Washington, with a continuation of the Nebraska projects.

Navajo Community College founded in Tsaile, Arizona.

President Lyndon B. Johnson directs the BIA in March to establish advisory school boards at all federal Indian schools.

1969 BIA implements Project T.R.I B.E. to yield considerable school control to Indian communities and tribes and issues school board handbook.

The U.S Senate released the Special Senate Subcommittee Report on Indian education entitled <u>Indian Education: A National Tradgedy--A National Challenge.</u> The report concluded that there had not been much progress in Indian education in the previous fifty years, and it prompted the passage of Public Law 92-318, Indian Education Act of 1972 (amended in 1974 and 1978).

1970 Ramah High School opened at Ramah, New Mexico.

The National Study of Indian Education was conducted by Robert Havighurst and Estelle Fuchs.

The National Indian Education was formed in Minneapolis, Minnesota.

President Nixon announces an era of Indian control over decisions affecting Indians, including the field of education.

Haskell Institute becomes Haskell Indian Junior College at Lawrence, Kansas.

First National convocation of Indian scholars sponsored by the American Indian Historical Society held at Princeton, New Jersey.

1971 Coalition of Indian-Controlled School Boards, Inc., formed in Boulder, Colorado.

American Indian Scholarships, Inc., founded in Albuquerque, New Mexico by Indians to assist Indian graduate students in selected areas of study.

Lakota Higher Education Center established for the Oglala Sioux at Pine Ridge, South Dakota.

Sinte Gleska College Center created for the Rosebud Sioux at Rosebud, South Dakota

Hehaka Sapa College established for Indian students of many tribes at D-Q University, a joint Mexican-American and Indian institution, at Davis, California.

Southwest Indian Polytechnic Institute administered by the BIA opens in Albuquerque, New Mexico.

1972 Indian Education Act of 1972. U.S. Office of Education in HEW directed to special needs of all Indian students in public schools. Major components included: Part A was allocated to the public school system to serve the educational needs of American Indian and Alaskan Native students; Part B provided for exemplary and demonstration projects with priority given to Indian tribes and organizations, Part C provided funds for adult basic education. A controversial component of this legislation which broadened the definition of "Indian" as historically defined by the Bureau of Indian Affairs. The legislation also provided for the National Advisory Council on Indian Education, which provides program priorities and has overseeing responsibilities.

The American Indian Higher Education Consortium formed in Boulder, Colorado by members of the Boards of Regents of the new Indian community colleges.

Turtle Mountain Community College created at Belcourt, North Dakota for the Montana Chippewa Tribe.

Standing Rock Community College established for the Standing Rock Sioux Tribe at Fort Yates, North Dakota.

1973 National Advisory Council on Indian Education members appointed by President Nixon, under terms of the Indian Education Act of 1972.

American Indian Satellite Community College for the Omaha, Winnebag and Santee Tribes of Nebraska, opens at Norfolk, Nebraska.

1974 Navajo Community College facilities dedicated at Tsaile, Arizona marking completed construction of the first Indian-owned and operated college in North America.

Fort Berthold Community College Center opens at New Town, North Dakota for Mandan, Hidatsa, and Arickara Tribes.

Sisseton-Wahpeton Community College opens at Sisseton, South Dakota.

1975 The Indian Self-Determination and Education Assistance Act.

1977 American Indian Policy Review Commission (P.L. 93-580, 88 stat., 1910-1914).

1978 NACIE supports priority be given to Indian-controlled institutions of higher education.

NACIE supports Indian tribes in the State of Maine in their self-determination efforts.

1979 Chemawa Boarding School builds a new campus.

1980 Chemawa celebrates its 100th birthday.

DEFINE

INTRUSION
MODES:
ORAL:
FORMAT:
ALLOTMENT:
HUMANITY:
RATIFIED:
PRIMITIVE:
RESERVATION
APPROPRIATIONS:
COMPETENT
ASSIMILATIONIST
STATUTE·
INTERPERSONAL.
INNOVATION·
TERMINATION:
REGRESSIVE:
CONCURRENT:
RESOLUTION:
CONTROL:

STUDY QUESTIONS

1. Briefly describe the following periods of history as mentioned in this unit.

   Mission Period.

   Treaty Period:

   Allotment Period

   Meriam Report and New Deal Period:

   Termination Period:

   Contemporary Period:

2. What did these particular legislative acts accomplish?

   1. Indian Reorganizaton Act:

   2. Johnson-O'Malley Act·

   3. House Concurrent Resolution 108:

3. How has the contemporary period of Indian education differed from the termination era?

4. Describe the Indian Educaiton Act of 1972 and indicate the extent to which it impacted schools in America

5. To what extent do you believe that American Indians are gaining control of their education?

6. Are Indian tribes in your area developing curriculum about their particular tribe?

7. What are the advantages of American Indians making decisions regarding their own educational future?

Footnotes

1. U.S. Congress, National Advisory Council on Indian Education, "First Annual Report," p. 106.

2. Hagan, William T., "Nineteenth Century Indian Education Programs," Clash of Cultures, p. 98.

3. Same as #2.

4. Schierbeck, Helen M., Misiaszek, Lorraine, and Barlow, Earl, American Indian Policy Review, p. 13.

5. Hagan, Clash of Cultures, page 99.

6. Hagan, Clash of Cultures, page 100.

7. Havighurst, Robert J., and Fuchs, Estelle, To Live on This Earth, p. 224.

8. Same as #6.

9. Szasz, Margaret, Education and the American Indian, p. 38.

10. Szasz, Education and the American Indian, p. 66.

11. Szasz, Education and the American Indian, p. 66.

12. U.S. Congress, "National Advisory Council," p. 134.

13. U.S. Congress, "National Advisory Council," p. 109.

14. U.S. Congress, "National Advisory Council," p. 110.

15. U.S. Congress, "National Advisory Council," p. 260.

16. U.S. Congress, "National Advisory Council," p. 273.

17. U.S. Congress, Senate, The Study of the Education of Indian Children, p. 17.

18. Same as #17.

Footnotes, Chapter 2

19. Coombs, Madison L. *Educational Disadvantages of the Indian*, p. 105.

20. Havighurst, *Life on This Earth*, p. 318.

21. Havighurst, *Life on This Earth*, pp. 17-18.

22. U.S. Congress, "National Advisory Council," pp. 94-95.

CPSIA information can be obtained
at www.ICGtesting.com
Printed in the USA
BVHW012148080422
633864BV00002B/14